Reading SATs Catch-up
Ages 10–11

KS2 Year 6 — Catch-up

Boost your results with targeted preparation for the Year 6 SATs

Published in the UK by Scholastic, 2016

Scholastic Distribution Centre, Bosworth Avenue, Tournament Fields, Warwick, CV34 6UQ

Scholastic Ireland, 89E Lagan Road, Dublin Industrial Estate, Glasnevin, Dublin, D11 HP5F

SCHOLASTIC and associated logos are trademarks and/or registered trademarks of Scholastic Inc.

www.scholastic.co.uk

© 2016, Scholastic

3 4 5 6 7 8 9   3 4 5 6 7 8 9 0 1 2

A CIP catalogue record for this book is available from the British Library.

ISBN 978-1407-16079-5

Printed and bound by Ashford Colour Press Ltd, Gosport, Hampshire, PO13 0FW

Paper made from wood grown in sustainable forests and other controlled sources.

All rights reserved. This book is sold subject to the condition that it shall not, by way of trade or otherwise, be lent, hired out or otherwise circulated without the publisher's prior consent in any form of binding or cover other than that in which it is published and without a similar condition, including this condition, being imposed upon the subsequent purchaser.

No part of this publication may be reproduced, stored in a retrieval system, or transmitted, in any form or by any means, electronic, mechanical, photocopying, recording or otherwise, other than for the purposes described in the content of this product, without the prior permission of the publisher. This product remains in copyright.

Due to the nature of the web we cannot guarantee the content or links of any site mentioned. We strongly recommend that teachers check websites before using them in the classroom.

Every effort has been made to trace copyright holders for the works reproduced in this book, and the publishers apologise for any inadvertent omissions.

Extracts from National Curriculum for England, English Programme of Study © Crown Copyright. Reproduced under the terms of the Open Government Licence (OGL). www.nationalarchives.gov.uk/doc/open-government-licence/version/3/

Author Graham Fletcher

Editorial Rachel Morgan, Anna Hall, Mary Nathan, Tracy Kewley

Cover and Series Design Neil Salt and Nicolle Thomas

Layout Claire Green

Illustration Paul Moran @ Beehive Illustration

Photographs Page 50: 'Triathlon participants', Jacob Lund/ Shutterstock.com; 'Rockclimber', Daxiao Productions/Shutterstock.com; 'Kite boarding', EpicStockMedia/ Shutterstock.com

Contents

How to use this book	4
Progress chart	5
Words in context: non-fiction	6
Words in context: fiction	8
Words in context: poetry	10
Retrieving information (1)	12
Retrieving information (2)	14
Retrieving key details	25
Summarising main ideas	28
Make inferences from the text	30
Explain and justify inferences (1)	32
Explain and justify inferences (2)	36
Explain and justify inferences (3)	38
Inference in poetry	40
Prediction	44
How information is related	46
How meaning is enhanced: language	48
How meaning is enhanced: structure	50
How meaning is enhanced: presentation	52
Making comparisons	54
Fact and opinion	56
Question types: selected	58
Question types: short answer	60
Question types: long answer	62
Test skills	64

How to use this book

This book will help you with what you need to know before you take the National Tests.

You can check the answers at **www.scholastic.co.uk/boosteranswers.**

The title of the topic.

What you should be able to do after you complete this page. You can tick off each one as you can do it.

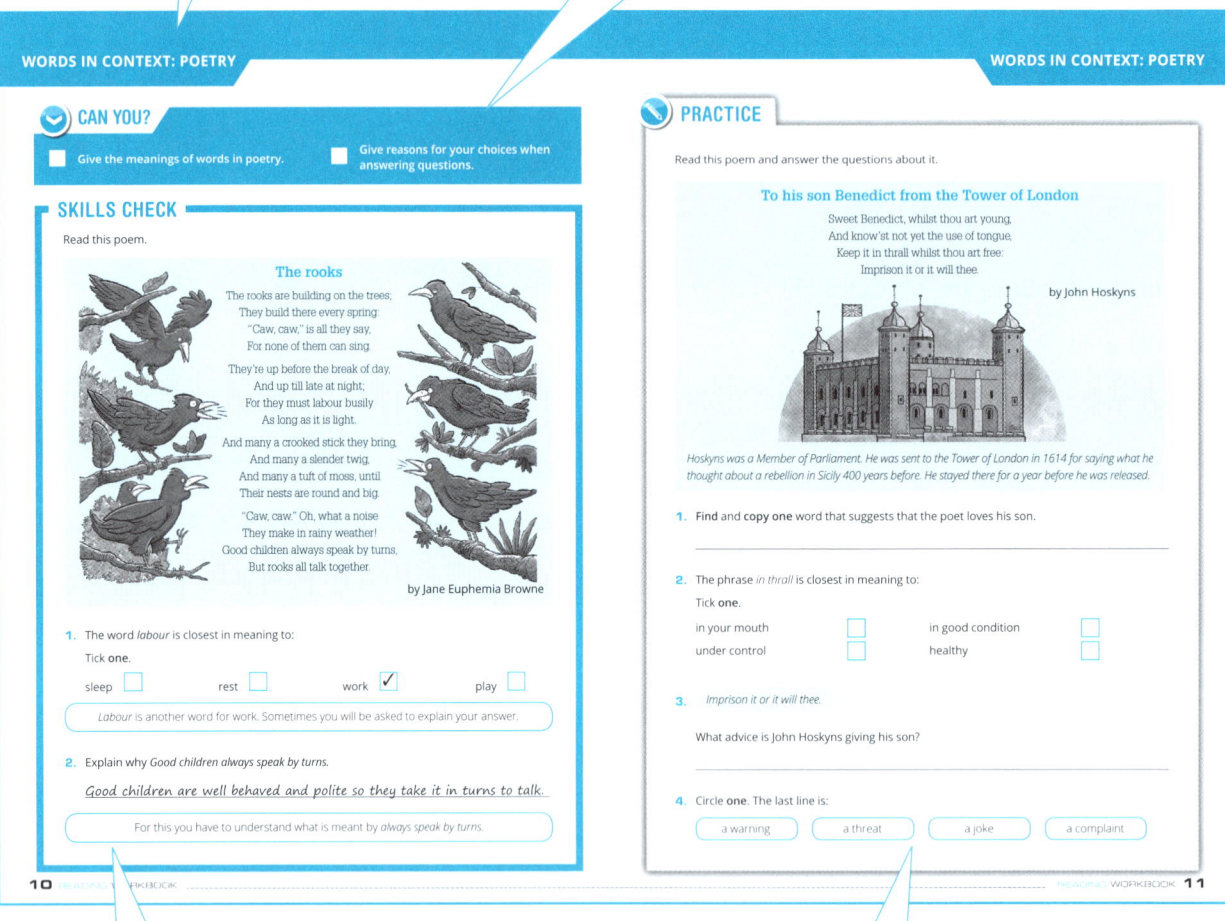

Skills check provides some background information on the topic to help you answer the questions.

Complete the practice questions to check your learning.

Progress chart

Topic	Revised	Practised	Achieved
Words in context: non-fiction			
Words in context: fiction			
Words in context: poetry			
Retrieving information (1)			
Retrieving information (2)			
Retrieving key details			
Summarising main ideas			
Make inferences from the text			
Explain and justify inferences (1)			
Explain and justify inferences (2)			
Explain and justify inferences (3)			
Inference in poetry			
Prediction			
How information is related			
How meaning is enhanced: language			
How meaning is enhanced: structure			
How meaning is enhanced: presentation			
Making comparisons			
Fact and opinion			
Question types: selected			
Question types: short answer			
Question types: long answer			

WORDS IN CONTEXT: NON-FICTION

CAN YOU?

- [ ] Give the meanings of words in non-fiction.
- [ ] Give reasons for your choices when answering questions.

SKILLS CHECK

Remember: Words often have more than one meaning. You have to pick the one that fits into the passage you are reading. Sometimes the answers will be more than one word long.

This piece of writing is about a large army attacking a neighbouring country. To find the answer, read the text, read the question and try to work out which option fits into it the best.

The Battle of Banicor

Margon the Mean, the ruler of the entire western part of Asigovia, looked round her. She was pleased. She had assembled a huge army of warriors and was now in a position to make her attack on Nostrovia.

1. Find and copy the word that tells us that Margon was merciless.

   mean

> The questions come in the order of the answers in the text. This is question 1 so the answer will be near the beginning of the story. Margon is a military leader who is about to attack another country so **mean** is the most likely answer.

2. *She had **assembled** a huge army of warriors ...*

   In this sentence, the word *assembled* is closest in meaning to:

   Tick **one**.

   joined. [ ]   gathered. [✓]   constructed. [ ]   met. [ ]

> If you know what **assembled** means, the question is easy. If you don't, you will have to try to work it out. All of the choices have some links to **assembled** but they don't all fit into the context in which it is being used. If you are not sure which is the best fit, try putting each of them into the sentence.

WORDS IN CONTEXT: NON-FICTION

PRACTICE

Margon's soldiers were well trained and carried the most sophisticated weapons. Her spies had told her that the Nostrovian army was, in comparison, pitifully armed. Margon was confident of success. She was certain that her battle plan would be enough to destroy her enemies and she was convinced that this would be an easy victory.

1. Explain **two** things that the words *pitifully armed* suggest about the Nostrovian soldiers.
    1. There not very good wepons.
    2. Brocken wepons.

2. *Margon was **confident**.*

    Find and copy **two** more words from the story that show that Margon expected to win the battle.
    1. she was certain that her battle plan would win.
    2. She was convinced that this would be an easy victory.

WORDS IN CONTEXT: FICTION

CAN YOU?

☐ Give the meanings of words in fiction.

☐ Give reasons for your choices when answering questions.

SKILLS CHECK

Remember: Words often have more than one meaning. You have to pick the one that fits into the passage you are reading. Sometimes the answers will be more than one word long.

The Seeker explains

"Where are we?" asked James.

"Rebus. The former capital of the Underworld," answered the Seeker.

"Former?"

"Yes, there is no capital now. It is ruled by the forces of Grunhild from Castle Kilbader."

"Grunhild?" James hadn't a clue what the Seeker was talking about. It was like having a history lesson in some foreign language.

"Grunhild. Don't say it so loud. It's not safe to be heard mentioning his name. His spies are everywhere and his vengeance is swift. His power is unrivalled in the Underworld. Some have tried, all have failed. He is as rotten as a rattlesnake and as vicious as a viper."

"I see. Not a man to be messed with then."

"No. It is he you have come to remove."

"Oh, great."

From *Into the Underworld* by Graham Fletcher

1. The word *former* is closest in meaning to:

   Tick **one**.

   newest. ☐   previous. ✓   present. ☐   future. ☐

   > Use clues in the text to help you answer the question – 'there is no capital now' tells you it was previously the capital.

2. *Not a man to be **messed with**.*

   What does *messed with* mean in this sentence?

   _annoy_____

   > This question could be answered with a number of words. You need to look for a meaning that makes sense in the sentence.

WORDS IN CONTEXT: FICTION

PRACTICE

Read this passage and answer the questions about it.

A Cara is Born

A cold wind whipped across Briggs Brothers' Scrapyard. It drove harsh rain before it like machine-gun bullets. In the far corner, away from all of the other vehicles, Cara the Caravanette huddled silently, hoping the storm would soon blow over.

From *Cara the Caravanette* by Graham Fletcher

Glossary: A **caravanette** is another name for a motor-home.

1. *A cold wind **whipped** across Briggs Brothers' Scrapyard*

   What does the word *whipped* tell us about the way the wind moved?

   _____

2. *It drove **harsh** rain before it...*

   What does the word *harsh* tell us about the rain?

   _____

3. What does *like machine-gun bullets* tell us about what the rain felt like?

   It was hard.

   _____

4. *Cara the Caravanette **huddled** silently, hoping the storm would soon blow over.*

   Circle **one**. In this sentence, *huddled* is nearest in meaning to:

   (hunched)   (lay down)   (spread out)   (jumbled)

   As the four people walked round her, Cara watched them through her wing mirrors. They were definitely interested! She did her best to preen herself and look impressive but it only seemed to draw attention to her dented bodywork. Still, what did they expect from a forty-five year old Volkswagen?

5. **Find** and **copy one** word from that final paragraph that shows Cara is in poor condition.

   _____

WORDS IN CONTEXT: POETRY

CAN YOU?

- [ ] Give the meanings of words in poetry.
- [ ] Give reasons for your choices when answering questions.

SKILLS CHECK

Read this poem.

The rooks

The rooks are building on the trees;
They build there every spring:
"Caw, caw," is all they say,
For none of them can sing.

They're up before the break of day,
And up till late at night;
For they must labour busily
As long as it is light.

And many a crooked stick they bring,
And many a slender twig,
And many a tuft of moss, until
Their nests are round and big.

"Caw, caw." Oh, what a noise
They make in rainy weather!
Good children always speak by turns,
But rooks all talk together.

by Jane Euphemia Browne

1. The word *labour* is closest in meaning to:

Tick **one**.

sleep ☐   rest ☐   work ✓   play ☐

> *Labour* is another word for work. Sometimes you will be asked to explain your answer.

2. Explain why *Good children always speak by turns*.

<u>Good children are well behaved and polite so they take it in turns to talk.</u>

> For this you have to understand what is meant by *always speak by turns*.

WORDS IN CONTEXT: POETRY

PRACTICE

Read this poem and answer the questions about it.

To his son Benedict from the Tower of London

Sweet Benedict, whilst thou art young,
And know'st not yet the use of tongue,
Keep it in thrall whilst thou art free:
Imprison it or it will thee.

by John Hoskyns

Hoskyns was a Member of Parliament. He was sent to the Tower of London in 1614 for saying what he thought about a rebellion in Sicily 400 years before. He stayed there for a year before he was released.

1. **Find** and **copy one** word that suggests that the poet loves his son.

   _____

2. The phrase *in thrall* is closest in meaning to:

   Tick **one**.

   in your mouth ☐   in good condition ☐
   under control ☐   healthy ☐

3. *Imprison it or it will thee.*

   What advice is John Hoskyns giving his son?

   _____

4. Circle **one**. The last line is:

   (a warning)   (a threat)   (a joke)   (a complaint)

RETRIEVING INFORMATION (1)

CAN YOU?

☐ Find information.

SKILLS CHECK

Read this text and then read the question.

The Maldives

If you want to go to Paradise, go to the Maldives. These beautiful islands lie in the warm waters of the Indian Ocean, south west of India and Sri Lanka.

1. Where are the Maldives? Tick **one**.

In Paradise	☐	In the Indian Ocean	✓
South west of Africa	☐	South east of India and Sri Lanka	☐

> Read the text again and you will see that the answer has to be *In the Indian Ocean*. Although India and Sri Lanka are mentioned in the text, it says *south west* and the option says *south east*.

Sometimes the information you have to find will be in a table or a diagram. The table below shows the average temperatures and rainfall for each month in the Maldives.

	Jan	Feb	Mar	April	May	June	July	Aug	Sept	Oct	Nov	Dec
Temp °C	27	28	29	29	28	28	28	28	27	27	27	27
Rain mm	74	50	73	133	215	170	148	188	250	220	200	233

2. Put a tick in the correct box to show whether each of the following statements is **true** or **false**.

	True	False
June is the coldest month.		✓
September is the wettest month.	✓	
February is the driest month.	✓	
March and April are the hottest months.	✓	

> In this question, you have to get all four right to get 1 mark.

12 READING WORKBOOK

RETRIEVING INFORMATION (1)

PRACTICE

Read the text and answer the questions about it.

> From the air, the Maldives look like green spots on the ocean. The seaplane is only large enough for twelve passengers and their luggage. It is very noisy and not very comfortable. It drops down quickly to land on the water where a waiting boat takes you to your glorious island destination.
>
> Getting out of the plane, your face will break into a huge smile. Once ashore, you won't need shoes for the rest of your stay. There are no roads and only sandy paths link your room to the beach.

1. Circle the correct option to complete the sentence below.
   From the air the Maldives look like:

   green dots   green pots   green spots   green sprouts

2. Put a tick in the correct box to show whether each of the following statements is **true** or **false**.

	True	False
The seaplane can carry twelve passengers.		
The seaplane is very noisy.		
The seaplane is very comfortable.		
The seaplane drops down quickly to land on the water.		

3. Tick the correct answer to complete this sentence.

   Your face will:

   make a frown ☐   drop ☐   break into a smile ☐   light up ☐

4. Draw lines to make **two** facts about the islands.

   On the islands
   - you will need shoes.
   - the only transport is seaplane.
   - there are no roads.
   - sandy paths link your room to the beach.

RETRIEVING INFORMATION (2)

 **CAN YOU?**

☐ Find information.   ☐ Copy accurately.

SKILLS CHECK

Remember: Answers to retrieval questions are never long and are often only one word.

Flying for the first time

I don't really count the first time I flew as being a real flight. It was at Skegness. We were on holiday there. None of my family had ever flown and my dad decided it was time that we did.

1. Where did the writer go on holiday?

   Skegness

> The questions are always in order of where the answers appear in the text. So the second answer will always come after the first one in the text. To find the answer to the second question, read it and then continue reading the text from where you found the first answer.

2. How many of the family had flown before?

   None

3. Who decided that it was time that the family flew?

   Dad

RETRIEVING INFORMATION (2)

PRACTICE

Read the next part of the text and answer the questions about it.

> The 'airport' was a field just outside the town. There was a sign at the gate, which said: 'Pleasure flights here today'. At the far end of the field, a blue single-engined plane was waiting.

1. Whereabouts in the field was the plane?
   _____

2. What colour was the plane?
   _____

> We crowded into the plane. It was very small and I had to sit on my mum's knee. The engine roared and the propeller spun. Slowly, we bumped across the field. Then faster and faster! Suddenly, my stomach seemed to be in my mouth. I looked outside and we were up!
>
> We flew straight to Skegness and then right down the promenade. We turned round at the big clock and made our way back. I thought it was the most wonderful thing I had ever done. It was all over in less than ten minutes but my excitement lasted a lot longer.

3. Where did the writer sit?
   _____

4. Where did the plane turn round?
   _____

5. How long did the ride last?
   _____

RETRIEVING INFORMATION (2)

PRACTICE

Read the text and answer the questions.

8 June

Hello Diary,

I'm sorry I haven't written in you since May but I've been very busy planning my holiday to Greece. Now it's less than two weeks away. There is so much to do. I have to buy some sun cream, sunglasses and a new swimming costume. I'll go out tomorrow to do that.

9 June

Hello Diary,

Well that was a waste of time. The shop didn't have anything I wanted. I'll try again later in the week.

12 June

Hello Diary,

I've got the costume and the sunglasses but still no sun cream. At this rate I'll have to rub butter on me instead.

16 June

Hello Diary,

I've got the sun cream! Now I've just got to find the tickets, my passport and my Euros.

18 June

Goodbye Diary.
Greece here I come!

1. Circle the date on which the diary starts.

   6 June   8 June   16 June   18 June

2. Draw lines to match the writer to things that had to be bought.

   Writer — some sun cream / sunglasses / a passport / Euros / a new swimming costume

3. What did the writer think that she might have to use instead of sun cream?

   _____

4. Give **two** things the writer needed to find.

   1. _____
   2. _____

RETRIEVING INFORMATION (2)

PRACTICE

Read the text and answer the questions.

The Battle of Hastings

It was the best of times, it was the worst of times
1066 started so well for Harold but it ended so badly. How? It all started with the death of King Edward the Confessor in January of that year. It seems that he offered the English crown to Harold. Like modern monarchs, Harold was crowned King of England in Westminster Abbey.

What could possibly go wrong?
Lots!
In France, William of Normandy had eyes on the throne himself. Now that Harold was king, there was only one way that William could take the crown. He would have to defeat Harold in battle. He decided on an invasion plan and raised an army. Unfortunately for Harold, nobody told him!

Could it get any worse?
Yes!
The king of Norway, Harald Hardrada, also had plans. He wanted to recreate the Viking kingdom of Northumbria. In May 1066, the Norwegians invaded. Harold's army defeated them and sent them home. Unfortunately, Harold's army was made up of peasant farmers who needed to go back to their homes for the harvest. That meant that by August 1066, Harold hadn't got an army any more.

So what happened to William?
Nothing!
He watched and he waited.
On 20 September 1066, Harald Hardrada invaded again. He sailed up the River Ouse towards York, with more than 10,000 men. This was bad news for Harold! He got as many men as he could and raced north. They marched over 180 miles in four days and then took on the Norwegians at the Battle of Stamford Bridge. Amazingly, Harold won.

Was this when William made his move?
Yes!
William landed near Hastings, forcing Harold to race back from York to fight him. Harold had 5000 tired men. William had 15,000 fresh ones. The result was predictable.

1. When in 1066 did Edward the Confessor die?

RETRIEVING INFORMATION (2)

PRACTICE

2. Where was Harold crowned King of England?

   _____

3. Read the section headed *What could possibly go wrong?*

   What would William have to do to become King of England?

   _____

4. Harald Hardrada was the king of which country?

   _____

5. What did Harald Hardrada want to recreate?
   Tick **one**.

The kingdom of Heaven ☐	The kingdom of Fife ☐
The Viking kingdom of Northumbria ☐	The kingdom of Norway ☐

6. Why did the English army need to go home?

   _____

   _____

7. How many men came with Harald Hardrada for the second invasion?

   _____

8. How many miles did the English army march to York?

   _____

9. In which battle did Harold defeat the Norwegians?

   _____

10. Harold had 5,000 men but William had:
    Circle **one**.

    (10,000)   (15,000)   (20,000)   (25,000)

RETRIEVING INFORMATION (2)

PRACTICE

Read the text and answer the questions on it on page 20.

Mont Blanc

Towering over the small French town of Chamonix, close to the borders with Italy and Switzerland, Mont Blanc is a very impressive sight. In English its name means White Mountain, which is very appropriate because that's exactly what it looks like. At nearly 5000 metres, it is the highest mountain in Western Europe. It is so tall that it has snow covering it all year round.

Climbing Mont Blanc

Amazingly, Mont Blanc was first climbed in 1786. That's over 200 years ago. The mountaineers must have found it very difficult without today's modern climbing equipment and thermal clothing. Since then it has been climbed countless times. Over 20,000 climbers make it to the top each year nowadays.

Easier ways up

There is a cable car that goes from Chamonix. It doesn't actually go to the top of Mont Blanc but it takes you nearly 4000 metres up to the Aiguille de Midi, which means the Needle of the Midday. From there it is possible to walk to the summit. As the cable car lifts you quickly and easily over the white slopes, you are able to see the tents of some climbers who have stopped overnight half way up. You can get out at the Aiguille du Midi or you can carry on. However, if you stay on the cable car, don't forget your passport as the next stop is Italy.

Other ways to Italy

A quicker way to Italy is to use the Mont Blanc tunnel. It is seven miles long and goes straight through the mountain.

Other things to do

If you visit Chamonix, you cannot avoid Mont Blanc. It dominates the landscape and makes you feel very small. It is a reminder of the power of nature but it is not the only attraction in the area. If you don't feel like strapping on climbing gear you can always walk on the lower slopes or go cycling. It is easy to hire a bike. In the winter you can ski. The ski lifts also run all year round, whisking you gently to the higher slopes without any effort. Chamonix itself is an interesting town where you will find lots of restaurants and shops. If you want to go further, it is an easy trip to Switzerland. Geneva is just over an hour away by car. There is so much to do around Mont Blanc that it is well worth a visit.

RETRIEVING INFORMATION (2)

PRACTICE

1. Tick the correct answer to complete this sentence.

   Mont Blanc is:

   Tick **one**.

   a small French town. ☐   close to Germany. ☐
   an impressive sight. ☐   in England. ☐

2. How tall is Mont Blanc?
   _____

3. In which year was Mont Blanc first climbed?
   _____

4. How many climbers reach the top of Mont Blanc each year nowadays?
   _____

5. Give **two** things you can do on the lower slopes.

   1. _____

   2. _____

6. When can you ski?
   _____

7. What will take you to the higher slopes without any effort?
   _____

8. Give **two** things you will find in Chamonix.

   1. _____

   2. _____

9. How long does it take to get to Geneva by car?
   _____

RETRIEVING INFORMATION (2)

PRACTICE

Read the text and answer the questions on it on page 22.

The Cutty Sark

The tea years

The Cutty Sark is one of the most famous names in British naval history. Built in 1869 in Scotland, she was first used as a tea clipper. Tea clippers were boats that were designed to carry heavy loads but still go fast in order to bring tea back from China to England, a journey that took over four months. She was never the fastest ship on the tea route but she was certainly one of the best looking. Her tea route years lasted until 1878.

The poor years

From 1878 onwards work was in short supply for the Cutty Sark. Competition from steamships that did not rely on the wind meant that the Cutty Sark lost its tea routes and needed to find other work. This was not easy. The opening of the Suez Canal made things more difficult as sailing ships were not able to use it. This meant that the steamships had a huge advantage over them in the time they took to come back from Africa and Asia.

The ship's owners had to take any work they could. The Cutty Sark carried coal, jute, castor oil and even mail in the next few years, sailing to Japan, China, Australia, New Zealand and the USA.

The woollen years

In 1883, the Cutty Sark started carrying wool from Australia to England. Despite being relatively old, the ship became the fastest on that route, completing the voyage 25 days quicker than other ships. For ten years, the ship was the fastest way to bring wool back from Australia. However, as with the tea route, steamships became more competitive, gradually overtaking the Cutty Sark. In 1895, the ship was sold to a Portuguese company for which she worked until the 1920s. Her name was changed and she went back to carrying whatever cargo could be found.

The present time

The Cutty Sark is now in a museum in London. Despite a terrible fire in 2007, she has been restored to perfect condition. Re-opened by the Queen in 2012, the ship can be seen every year as a major landmark on the London Marathon route.

RETRIEVING INFORMATION (2)

PRACTICE

1. Tick the correct answer to complete this sentence.

   The Cutty Sark was built in:

   Tick **one**.

   1866 ☐   1867 ☐   1868 ☐   1869 ☐

2. The Cutty Sark was:
   Circle **one**.

   a battleship   a tea clipper   a steamship   a submarine

3. Put a tick in the correct box to show whether each of the following statements is **true** or **false**.

	True	False
The Cutty Sark's first sailings were from China to England.		
The Journey from China to England took less than three months.		
The Cutty Sark was the fastest ship between China and England.		
The Cutty Sark stopped sailing from China to England in 1878.		

4. Read the section headed *The poor years*.
   Give **three** things the Cutty Sark carried during this time.

   1. _____
   2. _____
   3. _____

5. Draw lines to join the Cutty Sark to places it went to.

   The Cutty Sark   Australia
                         USA
                         Argentina
                         Japan
                         South Africa

6. Where is the Cutty Sark today?

   _____

RETRIEVING INFORMATION (2)

Read the text and answer the questions on it on page 29.

Stoneway Primary School
Clement Road
Birdsley
BS24 1EY
8 May 2017

Dear Parents and Guardians,

We are organising the annual school visit. This year we are very pleased to announce that we are going to Snowdonia in North Wales. We have hired Plas Bychan outdoor pursuits centre for five days – 3 July to 7 July. All accommodation and food will be provided but you may want to give your child a small amount of money – no more than £10 – to spend during the week.

The children will sleep in dormitories with six children in each room. If your child has any allergies or special food needs, please let us know before the visit.

Activities will include:

- Pony trekking
- Canoeing
- Potholing
- Hill walking
- White-water rafting

The cost of the trip is £199. If you would like your child to take part, please complete the form below and return it to me by 19 May. The deposit of £50 is due on that date as well.

Yours faithfully,

Angela Massey

Angela Massey
Head teacher

Reply slip:

I would like (name of child) .... to go on the school trip to Plas Bychan outdoor pursuits centre.

I enclose a cheque for £50 for the deposit.

.... has the following allergies:

.... has the following special food needs:

Name .... Signed ....

RETRIEVING INFORMATION (2)

 PRACTICE

1. What is the full name of the school organising the trip?
   _____

2. When was the letter sent out?
   _____

3. Where is Snowdonia?
   _____

4. Which outdoor pursuits centre will the school will be using?
   _____

5. What date does the trip start?
   _____

6. How much spending money are the children allowed to take?
   _____

7. How many children will sleep in each room?
   _____

8. How much deposit do parents and guardians need to pay? Tick **one**.

   £50 ☐   £99 ☐   £150 ☐   £199 ☐

9. Who wrote the letter?
   _____

10. Give **three** pieces of information that parents and guardians have to fill in on the reply slip.

    1. _____

    2. _____

    3. _____

RETRIEVING KEY DETAILS

CAN YOU?

☐ Find key details. ☐ Copy accurately.

SKILLS CHECK

Remember: The texts will be different but the questions will be similar. For retrieval answers, you will be asked: Who? What? When? Where? How many?

This poem helps you to remember how many days each month has.

Thirty days hath September,
April, June, and November;
February has twenty-eight alone.
All the rest have thirty-one,
Except a leap year – that's the time
When February's days are twenty-nine.

1. How many months have 30 days?

   Four

2. When does February have 29 days?

   In a leap year

Who has seen the wind?

Who has seen the wind?
Neither I nor you:
But when the leaves hang trembling,
The wind is passing through.
Who has seen the wind?
Neither you nor I:
But when the trees bow down their heads,
The wind is passing by.

By Christina Rossetti

3. How can we tell when the wind is passing? Give **two** ways.

   1. _The leaves hang trembling._

   2. _The trees bow down their heads._

RETRIEVING KEY DETAILS

PRACTICE

Read this poem and answer the questions.

The first tooth

Through the house what busy joy,
Just because the infant boy
Has a tiny tooth to show!
I have got a double row,
All as white, and all as small;
Yet no one cares for mine at all.
He can say but half a word,
Yet that single sound's preferred
To all the words that I can say
In the longest summer day.
He cannot walk, yet if he put
With mimic motion out his foot,
As if he thought he were advancing,
It's prized more than my best dancing.

By Charles and Mary Lamb

1. What is causing the *busy joy*?
   _____

2. How many rows of teeth does the writer have?
   _____

3. How much can the baby say?
   _____

4. What is *prized* more than the writer's *best dancing*?
   _____

5. Give **two** things that the writer can do better than the baby.
   1. _____
   2. _____

RETRIEVING KEY DETAILS

PRACTICE

Read this text and answer the questions.

> Mazzan had three friends: Mohammed, Izzy and Ronny. Mazzan liked to go fishing with his friends but Mohammed wasn't as keen because he never seemed to catch anything. Izzy had the best rod. Ronny had bought a new net and they used it to keep the fish in. At the end of each trip they always let the fish go.

1. What were the names of Mazzan's friends?
   _____

2. Find a phrase that explains why Mohammed wasn't as keen on fishing as the others.
   _____

3. Who had the best rod?
   _____

4. What was the net used for?
   _____

5. What happened to the fish at the end of each trip?
   _____

SUMMARISING MAIN IDEAS

CAN YOU?

☐ Find the main ideas.   ☐ Summarise the main ideas.

SKILLS CHECK

Remember: First you have to find the main ideas and then explain them in a few words. In the tests, you will be asked to summarise ideas from more than one paragraph.

Boris Becker

Boris Becker, a 17 year old German, who had only been a professional tennis player for a year, surprised everyone by winning the men's title at his first attempt in 1985. He was the youngest person to do this. He returned to Wimbledon to defend his title the next year and won again!

What are the main ideas?
- He was 17 when he won the Wimbledon title in 1985.
- He was the youngest person to win the Wimbledon title.
- He won again at Wimbledon in 1986.

> The main ideas all have two things in common – Boris Becker and Wimbledon.

1. Which of the following is a good alternative title to *Boris Becker*? Tick **one**.

   Tennis ☐   Winning at Wimbledon ☐

   Boris Becker's early years at Wimbledon ✓   A young Boris ☐

   > Why is the correct answer *Boris Becker's early years at Wimbledon*?
   > The other answers are all connected with individual parts of the text. *Tennis* is too vague. *Winning at Wimbledon* could be about anyone who has won there. *A young Boris* could have been about when he was a child. The correct answer is the one that **summarises** the main ideas.

2. Using information from the text, tick one box in each row to show whether the statement is **true** or **false**.

	True	False
It was unlikely that Boris Becker would win at his first Wimbledon.	✓	
Boris Becker was Russian.		✓
Nobody younger than Boris had won the Wimbledon men's title before.	✓	
Boris Becker played again at Wimbledon in 1986.	✓	

28 READING WORKBOOK

SUMMARISING MAIN IDEAS

PRACTICE

Read the text and answer the questions about it.

Vikings

Vikings attacked the north of England over 1200 years ago. The first invaders came to steal, but later others came to stay. One of their main settlements was in York. The Vikings called it Jorvik. It became a new kingdom with its own Viking king. The last king of Jorvik was Eric Bloodaxe.

1. What are the main ideas?

   1. _____
   2. _____
   3. _____

2. Which of the following is a good alternative title for *Vikings*? Tick **one**.

   Viking warriors ☐   Vikings in Scotland ☐
   Vikings in Jorvik ☐   Viking kings ☐

Read the text and answer the question about it.

Alice knew that this was her most dangerous mission so far. She was very scared as she crept up the path towards the old building. She slid underneath an open window and strained her ears.

Inside the building, two men were talking in low voices. They were planning a bank robbery for the following Tuesday. They would pretend to be workmen digging up the road. When they had dug down far enough, they would dig a tunnel under the bank walls and into the safe room. They would empty the safe and return through the hole in the road, jump into a waiting van and get away with the money.

Alice sat below the window and tried to make sure she could remember what they had said. When was it they said the raid would take place?

3. Using information from the text, tick **one** box in each row to show whether the statement is **true** or **false**.

	True	False
Alice is on a dangerous mission.		
The robbers would pretend to be mending the road.		
The robbers would dig a tunnel and escape in a van.		
Alice could remember when the raid was to take place.		

MAKE INFERENCES FROM THE TEXT

CAN YOU?

☐ Make inferences.

SKILLS CHECK

Remember: For some questions you will have to work out what the author is telling you. Others will ask you to explain your ideas using evidence from the text to prove your points. A lot of marks on the Reading paper are for making inferences. This means working out what the writer wants you to know but doesn't actually say.

> When I first met Sal, I thought she was charming, witty and very beautiful. It didn't take long for me to realise my mistake.

1. What is the writer telling you about Sal in the second sentence?

   She was very different from what the writer first thought.

   > We don't know what Sal is really like, just that the writer's opinion of her changed.

> Very soon I knew that we were not meant for each other. She talked all the time – mostly about herself. I began to think she wasn't interested in me.

2. What makes the writer think Sal was not interested in him?

   She only seemed to talk about herself.

   > The writer shows Sal is only interested in herself.

MAKE INFERENCES FROM THE TEXT

PRACTICE

Read these short texts and answer the questions about them.

Unless you are very rich or very talented, it is unlikely that you will ever have driven a Formula 1 racing car. Most people just don't get the chance even though everyone wants it. For a lucky few though, Formula 1 gives them the keys to an amazing lifestyle where huge rewards are on offer in return for the risks the drivers take.

1. Why don't most people get the chance to drive a Formula 1 racing car?

_____

2. Using information from the text, tick **one** box in each row to show whether each statement is a **fact** or an **opinion**.

	Fact	Opinion
Most people don't get the chance to drive Formula 1 cars.		
Everyone wants the chance to drive Formula 1 cars.		
Huge rewards are on offer.		
Formula 1 drivers take risks.		

Rani Mackeson, a retired Formula 1 driver, said:

"I was frightened every time I raced. I didn't take chances. Perhaps that's why I was never World Champion. At speeds approaching 200 miles per hour, every corner was an accident waiting to happen. It was really dangerous. I could have lost my life in any race. I enjoyed it at the time but I am glad to be out of it now."

3. Why didn't Rani take chances?

_____

4. Why does Rani think he was never World Champion?

_____

EXPLAIN AND JUSTIFY INFERENCES (1)

CAN YOU?

- [ ] Make inferences.
- [ ] Explain the reasons for your inferences.

SKILLS CHECK

Remember: The questions will always be in the order in which the answers appear in the text.

> Sal appeared on a television reality show. She won it! She got her own column in a magazine. It was about her, her life and her friends. I knew we were finished when she didn't mention me in her articles. Sal was very happy. She had found her perfect job.

1. How did the writer know that the relationship was finished?

   <u>The column was about Sal, her life and her friends. The writer wasn't in the articles so he knew that she didn't think that he was part of her life.</u>

   > You need both parts to get 2 marks. The first part is the evidence. The second is the inference.

Read this longer text.

> Inspector Dawson looked carefully at the crime scene in front of her. The kitchen door was wide open. Her feet crunched across broken glass from the door as she stepped inside and followed a trail of footprints leading to the living room.
>
> Inside the living room, the furniture was all upside down as if the intruder had been looking underneath it. There was a tall cupboard that was also open. Inspector Dawson stepped carefully between its contents, which covered the floor, and looked into the cupboard. She saw a small, open, empty safe.
>
> The Inspector headed back through the kitchen and outside. It was obvious what had taken place. Suddenly, she stopped and turned round. Something was wrong. The broken glass was outside the house!
>
> In an instant the Inspector's thoughts about what had happened changed. It was no longer just a clear-cut break-in. She took out her pocket book and drew a picture of the scene. She would need that later. She didn't want to miss anything. Then she reached in her pocket for her mobile phone and started taking pictures of the glass and the door. Finally, she switched her phone to recording mode and spoke into it.
>
> "43 Greenfield Park Road. Break-in. Check the criminal records of the owner."

> By the end of the story, we do not know exactly what has happened but the writer has given us lots of hints that things are not what they seemed at first.

EXPLAIN AND JUSTIFY INFERENCES (1)

SKILLS CHECK

We see the events through the Inspector's eyes. That means that we think what she thinks. The Inspector thinks it is *obvious what had taken place.* She uses the clues. So do we!

- There has been a burglary.
- The burglars broke in through the kitchen door.
- They were looking for something.
- A safe is empty.

How much of this do we know and how much do we **infer**?

	We know	We infer
There has been a burglary.		✓
The burglars broke in through the kitchen door.		✓
They were looking for something.		✓
A safe is empty.	✓	

The first three statements are all **inferences**. The writer hasn't actually told us any of them.

What inference do we make about the empty safe?

We infer that it was full before the burglary.
The writer doesn't actually say that, we just assume it's true because of the **context**.

Something was wrong tells us our inferences weren't right.
The broken glass was outside the house! tells us why.

The writer has made us infer that the burglars broke in through the kitchen door. If the broken glass is on the outside, it must have been broken from the inside.

What does that make us infer about the burglary?

In an instant the Inspector's thoughts about what had happened changed tells us the Inspector knows what has happened but we don't. We have to try to work it out. She draws a picture and takes photographs.

Why?

We infer that this is to help her remember.

Finally, the Inspector reminds herself to check on the criminal records of the owner of the house.

We infer that she thinks that the owner was involved in the burglary.

EXPLAIN AND JUSTIFY INFERENCES (1)

PRACTICE

Read the text and then answer the questions.

Alice and the Duchess

"You can't think how glad I am to see you again, you dear old thing!" said the Duchess, as she tucked her arm affectionately into Alice's, and they walked off together.

Alice was very glad to find her in such a pleasant temper, and thought to herself that perhaps it was only the pepper that had made her so savage when they met in the kitchen.

"When *I'm* a Duchess," she said to herself, (not in a very hopeful tone though), "I won't have any pepper in my kitchen *at all*. Soup does very well without – Maybe it's always pepper that makes people hot-tempered," she went on, very much pleased at having found out a new kind of rule, "and vinegar that makes them sour – and camomile that makes them bitter – and – and barley-sugar and such things that make children sweet-tempered. I only wish people knew that: then they wouldn't be so stingy about it, you know–"

She had quite forgotten the Duchess by this time, and was a little startled when she heard her voice close to her ear. "You're thinking about something, my dear, and that makes you forget to talk. I can't tell you just now what the moral of that is, but I shall remember it in a bit."

"Perhaps it hasn't one," Alice ventured to remark.

"Tut, tut, child!" said the Duchess. "Everything's got a moral, if only you can find it." And she squeezed herself up closer to Alice's side as she spoke.

Alice did not much like keeping so close to her: first, because the Duchess was *very* ugly; and secondly, because she was exactly the right height to rest her chin upon Alice's shoulder, and it was an uncomfortably sharp chin. However, she did not like to be rude, so she bore it as well as she could.

"The game's going on rather better now," she said, by way of keeping up the conversation a little.

"'Tis so," said the Duchess, "and the moral of that is: 'Oh, 'tis love, 'tis love, that makes the world go round!'"

"Somebody said," Alice whispered, "that it's done by everybody minding their own business!"

"Ah, well! It means much the same thing," said the Duchess, digging her sharp little chin into Alice's shoulder as she added, "and the moral of *that* is: 'Take care of the sense, and the sounds will take care of themselves.'"

From *Alice's Adventures in Wonderland* by Lewis Carroll

EXPLAIN AND JUSTIFY INFERENCES (1)

 **PRACTICE**

These questions are all about Alice and the Duchess.

1. Read the paragraph beginning *Alice was very glad*. Which word suggests that Alice's meeting with the Duchess in the kitchen might not have been a happy one?
   _____

2. Why does Alice not say *When I'm a Duchess* in a hopeful tone?
   _____

3. Give **two** reasons why Alice says she won't have pepper in her kitchen?

   1. _____

   2. _____

4. How does Alice think food affects children?
   _____

Read the paragraph beginning *Alice did not much like keeping so close to her.*

5. What does *she bore it as well as she could* tell us about Alice's attitude to the Duchess resting her chin on Alice's shoulder?
   _____

6. Why did Alice whisper *it's done by everyone minding their own business*?
   _____

7. How does the last paragraph suggest that the Duchess is not really listening to Alice?
   _____

EXPLAIN AND JUSTIFY INFERENCES (2)

CAN YOU?

- [ ] Make inferences.
- [ ] Explain the reasons for your inferences.

SKILLS CHECK

Remember: Read what the writer is telling you, then work out what the writer is making you think.

The Scorpion

It's easy to be a superhero.
All you need to succeed is:
- A secret power
- A secret identity
- A really cool name
- A colourful costume
- A terrible enemy or two… or three

If you can be invincible as well, you'll do fine.

1. How does this information show that it is not easy to be a superhero?

   Most of the things in the list are not easy to get.

   > By giving a list of things that most of us don't have, the writer is inferring that it is actually not easy. What is said and what is meant are two different things.

   The Scorpion was all of those things but he was dangerous as well. He stared intently at his computer screen and knew that something was wrong. He knew that he would work out what it was.

2. How does the Scorpion's name suggest that he is dangerous?

   Scorpions are poisonous.

   Across town, in a hidden laboratory, the evil Captain Von Deathtrap was giggling to himself about his latest fiendish plan. With one flick of a switch the entire world would be in his wicked power.

3. What do the words *evil*, *fiendish* and *wicked* make the reader feel about the Captain?

   The reader would be scared of him because he has so much power.

   > You would still get a mark if you put the opposite point of view, so long as you proved it:
   > _The readers would respect the Captain because he is ruthless._

EXPLAIN AND JUSTIFY INFERENCES (2)

PRACTICE

Read the rest of the story and answer the questions about it.

Suddenly a red light flashed on the Scorpion's screen. He had found the Captain's hidden location! His Gyrowatch set the coordinates and came up with a route. Estimated time: six minutes.

The Scorpion's computer linked into the Captain's hideout. Now he could hear the villain laughing loudly.

"Seven minutes! Seven minutes until I push the button and rule the world!"

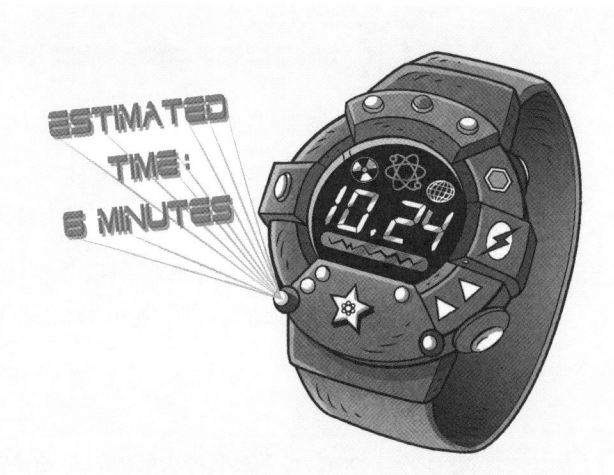

It would be close! The Scorpion would need his eight-wheeled Scorpio-copter to get there in time.

The Scorpio-copter skimmed the city. Five minutes gone! No time to knock on the door, just crash straight through it!

The door splintered and split, revealing Captain Von Deathtrap.

"Get back or I'll press the button!"

"Don't do it, Von Deathtrap. Don't make me use my secret weapon."

"You have no secret weapon. Do you think I am scared of your puny claws, Scorpion-boy?"

"No, not my claws but you should be worried about the taser in my tail."

With a flick of his tail, 50,000 volts shot across the room, knocking the Captain off his feet and leaving him helpless.

"Another villain who forgot there's a sting in the tail."

From *The Scorpion's First Tale* by Graham Fletcher

1. Who is this story aimed at? Tick **one**.

   people who like do-it-yourself books ☐   people who like cookery books ☐

   people who like furniture books ☐   people who like action storybooks ☐

2. *"Do you think I am scared of your puny claws, Scorpion-boy?"*

   Use information from the text to explain what the Captain thinks of the Scorpion.

   _____

   _____

EXPLAIN AND JUSTIFY INFERENCES (3)

CAN YOU?

☐ Make inferences.   ☐ Explain the reasons for your inferences.

SKILLS CHECK

Remember: Use the clues to help you work out what the author wants you to know.

Sharks

Sharks – the very word fills you with fear. Sleek, swift and silent, these deadly killers slice through the water, snapping their victims with their powerful jaws. If the lion is the king of the jungle, sharks are the rulers of the ocean.

1. Sharks are described as *Sleek, swift and silent*. Why might this fill you *with fear*?

   Sharks move quickly and you would not hear that they were coming.

2. Read the sentence beginning *Sleek, swift and silent*. Explain how this sentence supports the idea that sharks are strong creatures.

   The sharks must be strong to slice though the water

   or The sharks have powerful jaws.

3. How does comparing sharks to lions help the reader to understand how powerful sharks are?

   1. _Lions are very strong, so sharks must be too._

   2. _The lions are the kings of the jungle, so they are above all of the other animals. This means the sharks must be the same in the sea._

You are unlikely to be attacked by a shark. Shark attacks are rare. The vast majority of sharks are harmless to humans. On average, fewer than five people a year die from shark attacks.

4. How does this paragraph make it seem unlikely that we will be attacked by sharks?

   It makes it seem like there are very few attacks.

   It explains that only a small number of sharks are dangerous.

   It shows that very few people die from shark attacks.

> You need two of the answers to get 2 marks. All three answers explain their reasons.

EXPLAIN AND JUSTIFY INFERENCES (3)

PRACTICE

Read the rest of the article and answer the questions about it.

> Professor Angela Jones of the San Francisco Shark Research Centre said: "Sharks get a really bad press. They have a terrible reputation but it's not justified. There are nearly 500 species of sharks but only about four types have ever been known to attack people. About a quarter of all shark attacks have been caused by people provoking the sharks. Generally, sharks are more scared of us than we are of them."
>
> Sharks may well have good reason to be scared of humans. An estimated 100 million of them are killed each year. They are eaten in countries all around the world. In addition, fishing is reducing their food supply and pollution is poisoning the waters in which they swim.
>
> Professor Jones continued: "This is not a good time to be a shark. If we don't do something quickly, there won't be any sharks. We are destroying where they live and what they eat. Sharks are important creatures and should be given the respect they deserve."

1. How does the writer try to persuade us that most sharks are not dangerous?

   _____

2. Using information from the text, tick **one** box in each row to show whether each statement is a fact or an opinion.

	Fact	Opinion
Sharks get a really bad press.		
The sharks' reputation is not justified.		
There are nearly 500 different types of sharks.		
Sharks should be given the respect they deserve.		

3. How are human beings threatening sharks?

   _____

   _____

4. How can you tell that Professor Jones is an expert on sharks?

   _____

   _____

   _____

INFERENCE IN POETRY

CAN YOU?

☐ Make inferences from poetry.
☐ Explain the reasons for your inferences.

SKILLS CHECK

Making inferences about poetry is the same as making inferences about fiction or non-fiction.

PRACTICE

Read this poem and answer the questions about it on page 41.

From the dark side – beyond the night

1. Beyond the night, beyond the dawn,
lies the land where I was born;
a place no human's ever been,
a place no human's ever seen.

2. It's far away beyond the stars,
way past the Earth and way past Mars.
Out beyond the darkest night,
out of reach and out of sight.

3. I'll never see its sun again,
trapped here on Earth, the world of men.
My task is the planet to roam,
never to return to home.

4. My parents, wife and children gone,
I have no choice to carry on
And hide myself amongst the masses,
To watch and wait and see what passes.

5. I cannot tell them I am here,
For that would just ignite their fear,
And who quite knows what they might do
To someone whose real skin is blue?

6. For I have seen them with each other,
the things they do to one another,
the pain they cause, the terror they strike,
in those who do not look alike.

7. So I will sit and wait and hide
until this world lets me inside.
I do not know when that will be;
Far in future history.

by Graham Fletcher

INFERENCE IN POETRY

PRACTICE

1. How can we tell from the first verse that the writer does not come from Earth?
   _____

2. Read the second verse. Give **two** ways that we can tell that the writer comes from far away.
   _____

3. Why will the writer never see its planet's sun again?
   _____

4. What might have happened to the writer's family?
   _____

5. If humans saw the writer, why might it *ignite their fear*? Give **two** reasons.

   1. _____

   2. _____

6. Why does the writer not contact the humans?
   _____
   _____

7. Using information from the poem, tick **one** box in each row to show whether each statement is **true** or **false**.

	True	False
The writer can go home easily.		
The humans would be happy to meet the writer.		
The writer does not look like a human being.		
Humans treat each other well.		

8. What does the last line tell us about when the world will let the writer inside?
   _____

READING WORKBOOK **41**

INFERENCE IN POETRY

PRACTICE

This poem warns about the dangers of crossing busy roads.

James (for Hilaire Belloc)

1. I once saw James, the little toad,
Get run over in the road.
He had no time to swear or cuss,
As he was flattened by a bus!
Onlookers sighed, their heads a-tossing,
"He should have gone and used the crossing!"

2. Now he lies full six feet under.
How he feels, we can but wonder.
Down with the mud and young tree shoots
His coffin hugged by older roots,
Does he regret what he has done,
In taking on the 'chicken run'?

3. On tombstone, grey, his mother pasted
"My son is gone. His life is wasted."
And every night the driver screams
At what he sees within his dreams.
And friends who watched him squashed that day,
Take more care with the games they play.

4. The moral of this story waits
For those who flee the high school's gates.
Don't rush to cross the road ahead,
Take time to look both ways instead
And never try to hold a car back,
Or you'll be next, embossed in tarmac.

by Graham Fletcher

Glossary
embossed: pressed
chicken run: a dangerous game involving running across the road in front of vehicles

INFERENCE IN POETRY

PRACTICE

These questions are all about the poem, *James*.

1. *I once saw James, the little toad,...*

   What does this tell us about the writer's attitude towards James?
   _____

2. Why should James have used the crossing?
   _____

3. Read the second verse. How does *taking on the chicken run* explain why James has been run over?
   _____
   _____

4. Read the third verse. What might the driver see within his dreams?
   _____

5. What effect has James' death had on his friends?
   _____

6. What is the message in the poem?
   _____

7. How do the last four lines of the poem try to persuade us to take care when crossing the road?
   _____
   _____

PREDICTION

CAN YOU?

☐ Say what might happen.

☐ Explain your predictions using evidence from the text.

SKILLS CHECK

Remember: Prediction is a lot like inference. Your prediction has to be a continuation of the story. It has to be realistic and possible. You have to be able to show this by giving evidence from the text to explain your reasons.

Gran's shopping trip

My gran walked to the shops yesterday. She put her house keys in her bag but did not realise that the bag had a large hole in the bottom of it.

1. What is likely to happen to the keys?

They will fall through the hole in the bag.

> This is quite likely as the keys would be small and the hole is large.

Gran went to the supermarket. She got quite scared because she felt she was being followed. As she walked home, she knew she was right. A boy was chasing after her!

"Stop!" he shouted, waving his fist in the air.

2. What is gran likely to do? Give a reason for your thoughts.

> This question is more difficult. There is one mark for the prediction and one for the reason.

Gran might:

Run because she thinks the boy is threatening her.

　　↑　　　　↑
（Prediction）（Reason）

Stop because she wants to see why he has been following her.

　　↑　　　　↑
（Prediction）（Reason）

PREDICTION

PRACTICE

Read the texts and answer the questions that follow them.

> Within a minute of the 999 call, the fire engine was on its way. It was only a short journey to the burning house – perhaps five minutes – but the driver still went as fast as possible, using the engine's blue lights and siren to warn other road users on the crowded streets.

1. Based on what you have read, what does the text suggest is likely to happen next?

_____

> The fire engine arrived at the house. A woman and her baby were at an upstairs window. Flames were licking at the window ledge. The woman was screaming for help. The fire engine pulled up outside the house and the crew jumped out. The hoses were connected almost instantly and the crew sprayed the flames with water. As the flames went out, a ladder was raised up to the window. Some of the fire officers went into the house through the front door, using their powerful hoses to spray the flames in front of them.

2. What is likely to happen to the woman and her baby?

_____

3. What is likely to happen to the fire downstairs? Give a reason for your answer.

_____

_____

> An ambulance arrived shortly afterwards. The paramedics examined the mother and the child. Apart from a few bumps and bruises, they were unharmed. They had been very lucky. The downstairs of the house had been badly damaged but they had managed to escape. However, as the mother looked back at the smoke-filled house, she knew that her troubles were not over. It would be a long time before things were back to normal.

4. Based on what you have read, what does the last paragraph suggest might happen to the mother and child next?

_____

_____

HOW INFORMATION IS RELATED

CAN YOU?

☐ Show where information is related. ☐ Explain how the information is related.

SKILLS CHECK

Remember: For these questions, you have to be able to find information throughout the text and show how it links together. Sometimes you will have to **find** and **copy** information. Sometimes you will have to put it in your own words. These questions will cover the whole of a text so they will come near the end of the questions on each text.

The Old Man of Storr

Despite what it sounds like, the Old Man of Storr is not a person at all. It is a tall lump of rock on the Isle of Skye in Scotland. It is a vertical pinnacle that can be seen from miles away and can only be climbed by experienced mountaineers.

Although you may not be able to get to the top of the Old Man, the same cannot be said for the Storr itself. This is the 700 metre high hill on which the Old Man sits. There is a walk to the top of the Storr that takes about an hour. The walk can be done in most weather conditions but it can be muddy when it is wet.

The first stage of the walk along a gravel path is easy. The slope is gentle and the path is good. The higher part of the walk, close to the Old Man, becomes much more difficult because it is very steep and the path is much rougher. Not everyone will be able to do this part.

1. The walk starts easily. Find and copy a group of words that show that the walk becomes harder.

   The higher part of the walk, close to the Old Man, becomes much more difficult

   > This part of the paragraph marks the point where the easy part ends and the hard part starts.

2. What changes take place to make the walk harder?

   At the start the slope is gentle and the path is good.

   Later it is very steep and the path is much rougher.

3. Read the first and last paragraphs. How do they link together?

   The Old Man of Storr can only be climbed by experienced mountaineers so not everyone can do it. The last part of the walk cannot be done by everyone.

HOW INFORMATION IS RELATED

PRACTICE

Read the text and answer the questions.

> The number 10 bus goes on a circular route. It starts in the city centre and goes right round the outside of the city before returning to its starting point.
>
> During the week, it is always busy between the city centre and the hospital, particularly at visiting time. In the morning and late afternoon, the bus is full of children who attend Bore Hill secondary school. It's always very noisy and crowded then.
>
> At night, the bus is much quieter, especially as it makes its last journey back to the city centre.

1. Give **two** places where the bus is always busy.

    1. _____
    2. _____

2. Give **three** times when the bus is always busy.

    1. _____
    2. _____
    3. _____

3. Number the following events to show the order they happen in the text. The first one has been done for you.

The bus starts in the city centre.	1
The bus is much quieter.	☐
The bus is full of children.	☐
The bus makes its last journey back to the city centre.	☐
The bus is very noisy.	☐

4. When is it much quieter on the bus?

    _____

5. Read the first and last paragraphs. How do they link together?

    _____
    _____

HOW MEANING IS ENHANCED: LANGUAGE

CAN YOU?

☐ Identify and explain where language enhances meaning.

SKILLS CHECK

Remember: These questions are about how meanings are made clearer. It is not enough to be able to recognise what is happening. You have to be able to explain it.

The Eiffel Tower

The Eiffel Tower in Paris stands like a giant over the city, never asleep, always on guard. From its lofty summit, tiny people can be seen rushing between its massive feet.

1. Read the first paragraph. **Find** and **copy** a phrase that makes the Eiffel Tower seem human.

   always on guard

   > You would receive 1 mark for any phrase that makes the Eiffel Tower seem human, such as *never asleep* or *its massive feet*.

2. **Find** and **copy three** words that suggest how big the Eiffel Tower is.

   > You would get 2 marks for *giant*, *lofty* and *massive*. You would get 1 mark for any two of these.

In the dark

I am not scared of the dark. I am scared of what's in the dark. Anything could be out there in the gloom. What fearful creatures are hiding, waiting to pounce on me? It's always creepy in the dark. You must have felt something similar.

3. How does the writer build up the fear in the first two sentences?

   The first sentence shows the writer is not scared of the dark. The slight change to the second emphasises that the writer is scared of what is in the dark.

4. **Find** and **copy four** different words from the rest of the passage that suggest danger.

   > You would get 2 marks for any four of: *scared, gloom, fearful, hiding, pounce, creepy*. You would get 1 mark for any three of the above.

HOW MEANING IS ENHANCED: LANGUAGE

PRACTICE

Read the poem and answer the questions about it.

> Late lies the wintry sun a-bed,
> A frosty, fiery sleepy head;
> Blinks but an hour or two; and then,
> A blood-red orange, sets again.
>
> From *Winter time* by Robert Louis Stevenson

1. **Find** and **copy two** phrases that make the sun seem like a person.

    1. _____

    2. _____

2. *A blood-red orange...*

    How does this help the reader understand what the sun looked like?

    1. _____

    2. _____

Read this text and answer the questions about it.

> I always look forward to my birthday with mounting excitement. It reaches a peak on the day before when my wait seems like an eternity. When it is gone, my life is like a bucket with a hole in it, empty for another year.

3. How does the writer show how he or she looks forward to the birthday?

    _____

    _____

4. Circle **one** word which shows us that the writer feels that the birthday always takes a long time to arrive?

    (mounting)   (excitement)   (eternity)   (year)

5. Why does the writer compare the rest of the year to *a bucket with a hole in it*?

    _____

READING WORKBOOK **49**

HOW MEANING IS ENHANCED: STRUCTURE

CAN YOU?

☐ Identify and explain where structure enhances meaning.

SKILLS CHECK

Remember: The structure of a text includes: headings, subheadings and paragraphs.

PRACTICE

Calling all thrill seekers!
These are the top three blasts this year:

1. Make a splash

Get in the swim with an open-water challenge. The Lake District is a great place for this. There are lots of lakes and not many boats. The speed of the boats is limited so you might even overtake them.

It's not something for absolute beginners but don't worry if you've never tried it before. Specialist companies will lead you on guided swims across some of the most beautiful lakes in the country. Most people just do one lake but you can do three of four in a day if you're feeling strong enough.

2. Surf the skies

Kitesurfing – it lives up to its name! You fly across the waves pulled by a kite. The stronger the wind, the greater the thrill.

If you're a beginner, expect to spend more time in the water than on it. You'll probably need professional lessons before you go onto the water by yourself. Sunny weather and high temperatures always help so try going to Vietnam or Mauritius for this thrill.

3. Hang on in there

Climbing – that really is life on the edge! Just you and the rocks. What could be simpler? Be careful though. You could do this for nothing, but cheap isn't always safe. It's better to use a rope and a harness, but some people love the risk of free-climbing and just go for it. It's up to you how high you want to go.

You might think these are all too dangerous. What's the alternative? Sit at home and watch it on television? Listen to your friends tell you how good it was? They're all very safe and that's the problem.

HOW MEANING IS ENHANCED: STRUCTURE

PRACTICE

Read the text and then answer these questions.

1. Write down the heading of the text.
   _____

2. Do you think this is a good heading? Why?
   _____
   _____

3. Write down the **three** subheadings used in the text.

   1. _____
   2. _____
   3. _____

4. How do the subheadings help the reader?
   _____
   _____

5. What is the purpose of the final paragraph?
   _____
   _____

HOW MEANING IS ENHANCED: PRESENTATION

CAN YOU?

☐ Identify and explain where presentation enhances meaning.

SKILLS CHECK

Remember: The presentation of a text includes: pictures and captions, diagrams, charts, text boxes and font choices (such as colour, *italics* or **bold**).

PRACTICE

Jam tarts

Ingredients
- 250g plain white flour
- 110g butter
- 60ml water
- Jam – whichever flavour(s) you prefer

Make these delicious jam tarts.

Method

1. Preheat the oven to 180°C or gas mark 4.
2. Put the flour in a bowl.
3. Cube the butter.
4. Rub the butter into the flour until it looks like breadcrumbs.
5. Pour a small amount of water in and start to bring the dough together. Keep adding small amounts of water until it binds together as a dough (you might need more or less water depending on the mix).
6. Wrap in clingfilm and put in the fridge for 20 minutes.
7. Take the chilled dough out of the fridge and roll it out on a lightly floured surface.
8. Use a round cutter to *carefully* cut out the pastry. Put the pastry discs into a greased tart tin.
9. Put a heaped teaspoon of jam into each case.
10. Bake for 10 to 15 minutes.
11. When you take them out of the oven the jam will be <u>really hot</u>. Leave to cool on a wire rack before tucking in!

HOW MEANING IS ENHANCED: PRESENTATION

PRACTICE

Read the jam tart recipe and then answer these questions.

1. Draw lines to match each feature to its purpose.

Feature
Bullet points
Italics
Numbers
Caption

Purpose
To give instructions.
To give more information.
To list key points.
To emphasise text.

2. Why are the words *really hot* underlined?

   _____

3. Why is some of the text in a box?

   _____

4. How does the picture help the reader?

   _____

MAKING COMPARISONS

CAN YOU?

☐ Make comparisons to show how things are similar or different in a text.

☐ Explain how meaning is enhanced.

SKILLS CHECK

Remember: These questions usually cover the whole of the text. You may be asked to show how something has changed during the text, for example attitudes or emotions. You could be asked to compare different people or places.

Sadie's birthday cards

Sadie was very excited. It was her birthday and she was eagerly anticipating receiving lots of cards. The postman didn't come at his usual time! She waited nervously, anxiously watching out of the window. Just when she had given up all hope, he appeared.

"Sorry, Sadie," he said. "I got a puncture. Here you are."

She beamed with pleasure when she saw the huge pile of cards in his hand.

1. How does Sadie's mood change?

   At the start of the text, Sadie is very excited. When the postman didn't come on time, she became nervous. At the end, she was very pleased.

   > To get 2 marks, you have to show how Sadie's mood changed and give examples of it from the text. You would only get 1 mark for saying she was excited at the start and happy at the end.

The car park

Five years ago, there was a car park at the end of our street, which we all hated. It was very bumpy and covered with broken glass. Now it has been made into a beautiful garden that everyone can enjoy.

2. Compare the area that was the car park at the start and the end of the text.

   At first it was bumpy and covered with broken glass.

   At the end it was a beautiful garden.

3. How did people's attitudes change towards the area?

   At first they hated it but at the end they all enjoyed it.

MAKING COMPARISONS

PRACTICE

My school changed its uniform this year. We used to have to wear ties but now we wear sweatshirts instead.

1. How has the school uniform changed?
   _____

My sister, Michelle, has a fiery temper. She looks for arguments and is happiest when everyone else is miserable. My brother, Troy, is quiet and friendly. He says he doesn't like arguments but always joins in when Michelle starts. Together, they often pick on me. I think it is bullying but my mum says it is part of growing up in a family and they will soon stop.

2. Compare Michelle and Troy.
   _____
   _____
   _____
   _____

3. How are the attitudes of the mother and the writer different?
   _____
   _____

Caravans

Early caravans	Modern caravans
Horse drawn	Towed by cars
Wood stoves	Central heating
Oil lamps	Electric lighting

4. How has the type of lighting in caravans changed?
   _____

FACT AND OPINION

CAN YOU?

☐ Identify a fact.   ☐ Identify an opinion.

SKILLS CHECK

Remember: Facts are true and can be proved. Opinions are what someone thinks or believes and may not be true.

Life in the fast lane

I first went to a tenpin bowling alley when I was about eight years old. I was awestruck by the size of the place. It was as big as an aircraft hangar – 24 lanes stretched out in front of me. I loved the noise: the crash of the pins; people shouting with delight; the loud music.

I was hooked as soon as I played my first game. It looks simple but it's not! I love the challenge of keeping the ball in the lane and wiping out the pins at the other end. There's no better feeling than watching them all fall over. The balls come in various weights and you can even use a ramp to help you if they are too heavy. Youngsters and beginners can score highly by using the 'bumpers'. These are barriers that stop the ball going into the gutter, so you score every time. Young and old alike can compete with each other. This has enabled me to get great pleasure from introducing my children and my grandchildren to the game.

The maximum score is 300. I play every week. I've never got it yet but who knows, one day perhaps?

1. Using information from the text, tick **one** box in each row to show whether each statement is a **fact** or an **opinion**.

	Fact	Opinion
It was as big as an aircraft hangar.		✓
There's no better feeling than watching all the pins fall over.		✓
The balls come in various weights.	✓	
The maximum score is 300.	✓	

> Read the text through carefully and think about whether what is being said is true (a fact) or what someone thinks (an opinion).

FACT AND OPINION

PRACTICE

Healthy eating

Everybody loves food. Children love fast food. Burgers, chips and nuggets all taste great. There are lots of takeaway shops, meaning that fast food is easy to buy. It isn't always good for you though. Lots of fast food contains large amounts of salt and fat. Salads are really healthy but some people think that they are boring. Healthy eating gives us energy and makes us grow strong. However, if you're busy, a takeaway once in a while won't do you too much harm.

1. Using information from the text, tick **one** box in each row to show whether each statement is a **fact** or an **opinion**.

	Fact	Opinion
Everybody loves food.		
There are lots of takeaway shops.		
Salads are really healthy.		
Burgers, chips and nuggets all taste great.		

The Titanic

Many people believe that the Titanic is the grandest ship ever built. It has captured the imagination of the public more than any other ship in history. Perhaps it is because it was described as 'unsinkable' by its designer. Perhaps because it sank on its first voyage. Perhaps because there is so much mystery surrounding its loss. Whatever the reason, it is certainly a fascinating ship!

2. Draw lines to show which of these statements about the Titanic are **facts**.

Fact

- It is the grandest ship ever built.
- It was described as 'unsinkable'.
- It sank on its first voyage.
- It is a fascinating ship.

QUESTION TYPES: SELECTED

CAN YOU?

☐ Answer questions by ticking, circling or drawing lines.

SKILLS CHECK

Some questions don't require you to write an answer, instead you need to tick a box, circle some text or draw lines.

My class

In my class there are seventeen boys and thirteen girls. We sit around tables. There are six people at each table. We haven't got a changing room so for PE, we get changed in the classroom. Then we go into the hall, which is near the playground. The best times are when we get to use the PE equipment.

1. In 'My class' there are:
Tick **one**.

thirteen boys ☐   fourteen girls ☐

sixteen girls ☐   seventeen boys ✓

> Make sure you read all of the choices carefully. The correct answer could be in any place. Read the text again. It's easy to confuse the numbers. There are thirteen girls and seventeen boys.

2. Circle **one**. The pupils get changed for PE in:

the changing room   (the classroom)   the hall   the playground

> Check the text carefully. All of the places are in it but the children get changed in the classroom because there isn't a changing room.

3. Put **one** tick in each row to show whether each of the following statements is **true** or **false**.

	True	False
The best times are when the children sit round tables.		✓
Six people sit around each table.	✓	
The hall is near the playground.	✓	
The best times are when the children use the PE equipment.	✓	

> All of the answers are in the text.

QUESTION TYPES: SELECTED

PRACTICE

Read this text about Saturn and answer the questions.

Saturn's rings were first seen by Galileo in 1610 through a telescope. However, Saturn is so big that it can be seen without a telescope if you know where to look. It is the sixth planet from the Sun. It has at least 50 moons! The largest moon, Titan, is larger than the planet Mercury.

Saturn itself has almost 100 times the mass of the Earth and is the second largest planet in the solar system. It is nearly 900 million miles from the Sun.

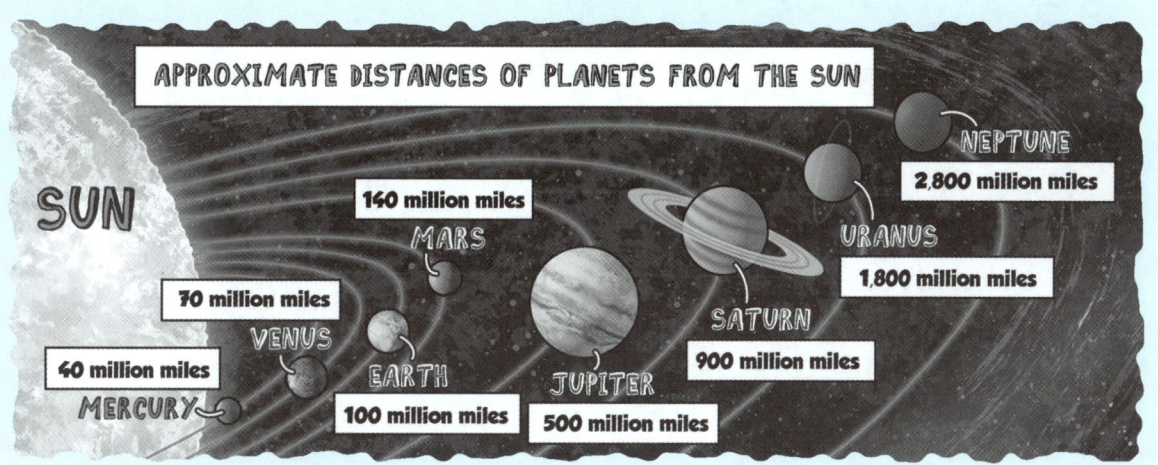

APPROXIMATE DISTANCES OF PLANETS FROM THE SUN

SUN
MERCURY — 40 million miles
VENUS — 70 million miles
EARTH — 100 million miles
MARS — 140 million miles
JUPITER — 500 million miles
SATURN — 900 million miles
URANUS — 1,800 million miles
NEPTUNE — 2,800 million miles

1. Who first saw Saturn's rings? Tick **one**.

   Da Vinci ☐   Galileo ☐   Mercury ☐   Shakespeare ☐

2. Draw lines to join Saturn to facts about it.

   Saturn
   - can be seen without a telescope.
   - is the sixth planet from the Sun.
   - has at least 118 moons.
   - has almost twice the mass of the Earth.
   - is the largest planet in the solar system.

3. How far is Jupiter away from the Sun? Tick **one**.

   About two hundred million miles ☐
   About three hundred million miles ☐
   About four hundred million miles ☐
   About five hundred million miles ☐

QUESTION TYPES: SHORT ANSWER

CAN YOU?

☐ Answer questions with short answers, referring to the text.

SKILLS CHECK

Some questions only require you to write a few words.

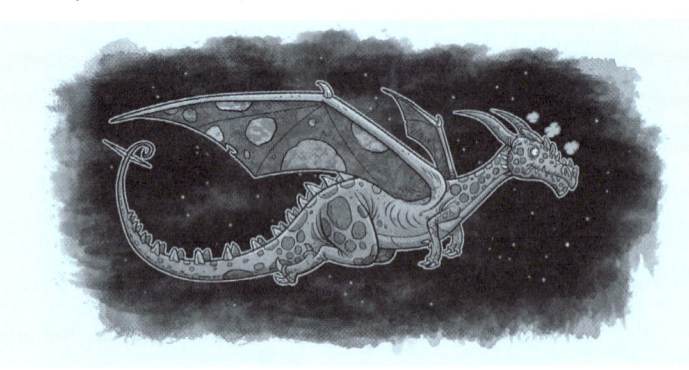

Dorca the dragon

Dorca the dragon flew across the night sky. Her quest was to find the secret of eternal dragon life. She knew that the knights of Nemore would try to stop her but she had dragon magic on her side!

1. Find and copy a phrase that shows that the extract is a myth.

   Dorca the dragon

   > There could be several answers here: *quest, knights of Nemore, secret of eternal dragon life, dragon magic*. The question only asks you to give **one** phrase. **Find** and **copy** questions will always require you to copy some words or sentence from the text.

The Tower of London

Sitting on the north bank of the River Thames, the Tower of London dates back almost a thousand years to William the Conqueror. At times it has been a palace, a stronghold and a prison.

2. Where is the Tower of London.

   On the north bank of the River Thames

3. How long ago was the Tower of London first built?

   Almost a thousand years ago

   > These questions also ask you to find answers in the text and to write a few words to answer them.

QUESTION TYPES: SHORT ANSWER

PRACTICE

Read the texts and answer the questions about them.

The storm

Rain tapped like ghostly fingers on my bedroom window. The wind battered the glass like an invader, threatening to break into my stronghold. I pulled the covers over my head. In my cocoon, I was protected from the world outside. As the storm eased, I forced my way out of my protective shell and made my way downstairs.

1. **Find** and **copy** a phrase that tells you what the rain sounded like.

   _____

2. What word does the writer use to describe the bed?

   _____

Scrubbitt's soap

You're guaranteed to be clean when you use Scrubbitt's. New and improved, this is our best-ever soap. You'll feel refreshed and smell wonderful. At only 49p you'll save money too!

3. **Find** and **copy four** phrases that are meant to persuade you to buy Scrubbitt's soap.

   1. _____
   2. _____
   3. _____
   4. _____

QUESTION TYPES: LONG ANSWER

CAN YOU?

☐ Answer questions with longer answers, referring to the text.

SKILLS CHECK

Some questions require you to write longer sentences or explanations.

Homeward bound

The wind bit at my overcoat, chilling me to the bone. It was midnight and I still had a mile to go. I trudged wearily in the direction of my house, feeling weaker with every step. It was out there in the darkness but I could not see it. I was beginning to despair as I felt I would not make it.

Suddenly, I saw it – a faint warm glow on the horizon. My mood lifted, my step lightened and I raced towards the house. I no longer noticed the cold or my tiredness. The snow stopped. The wind dropped. Within minutes I was inside, warm, dry and safe.

1. Explain how the writer feels in the two paragraphs with reference to the text.

   At the start, the writer is despairing because it says he 'trudged wearily' and is 'feeling weaker' but by the end he feels much happier as his 'mood lifted' and he was 'warm, dry and safe' inside.

2. Compare the wind in the first paragraph with the wind in the second paragraph.

   In the first paragraph the wind is very cold and strong as it says 'the wind bit at my overcoat, chilling me to the bone'. In the second paragraph, 'the wind dropped' so was no longer strong.

QUESTION TYPES: LONG ANSWER

PRACTICE

This text is about a boxing match.

The big match

In the blue corner was Mountain-Man Dan. He was huge. His arms bulged with muscles and his chest rippled every time he took a breath. He was the World Champion and everyone was afraid of him. He growled at the front row of the audience and everyone ducked.

In the red corner was the challenger, Hillbilly Haystack. Although he was a big man, he seemed tiny in comparison to Dan. He had only won the local championship and had nothing to lose. He didn't frighten people. He waved to his friends in the audience and they all waved back.

1. Look at the two men's names. What differences do they suggest about the men? Explain your answer.

   _____
   _____
   _____
   _____

2. Compare the reaction of the crowd to the two men.

   _____
   _____
   _____
   _____

READING WORKBOOK **63**

TEST SKILLS

CAN YOU?

☐ Understand the test paper.

SKILLS CHECK

Remember:

> You could be asked to look at fiction, non-fiction, poetry or drama. Remember that the text will be different, but the questions and how you answer them will be similar.

> The texts in the tests will usually be 600–700 words long.

> The questions will be in the order of the text – the answer to question 1 will come before the answer to question 2.

> Most of the marks will be for retrieval and inference questions – make sure you are comfortable answering these questions.

> Remember, the time for the test is for reading and answering the questions – make sure you don't run out of time.

What you should do if you can't find an answer:

- Go on to the next question and then go back to the text.
- Read the section that contains that answer and write it down on the test paper.
- Now read the section before that and see if the answer to the previous question is there.